DEAR READER!

What you hold in your discerning hands is the finest and highest quality comics magazine ON PLANET EARTH. All knowledgeable readers know that no comics periodical compares to **GOOD BOY MAGAZINE.**

ACCEPT NO FAKES!
ACCEPT NO IMITATIONS!
ACCEPT NOTHING LESS
THAN THE REAL THING!

We appreciate your commitment to QUALITY COMICS. Your purchase shouts to the world that you are a consumer who will not accept the trite, frail, NOTHING comics that the industry has taken to producing. So please, wash your hands, find a comfortable well-cushioned chair, and ENJOY!

With love,

MICHAEL SWEATER
EDITOR, BORN PROCRASTINATOR

BENJI NATE
LIL CUTIE

AND ALL OF...
The Good Boys!

This book was brought to you with the help of our patient and beautiful Kickstarter backers. There are none more pure or more smart. We love you.

Join us online at www.GoodBoy.zone!

"WHAT WAS THE WORST PART OF THE JOB?"

THAT'S A GOOD QUESTION.

SURE, WE LOOKED CUTE AND HAD SOME FUN...

...BUT IT WAS HARD WORK AND WE ALL SUFFERED A GREAT DEAL.

ALRIGHT, I THINK WE GOT IT!
THANK YOU FOR SPEAKING TO ME.
THANKS FOR THE COFFEE.

CLICK
SO, WHEN DOES THIS ARTICLE COME OUT?

WE'RE PLANNING TO FIT IT INTO NEXT MONTH'S MAGICAL GIRL ISSUE.
WE'RE STILL GATHERING UP A COUPLE LAST MINUTE INTERVIEWS.

NEWS
STAND
Enjoy!
COCONUT LIQUID

OH!

Girl Girl
MAGAZINE
THE MAGICAL EDITION
exclusive interviews
FORMER MAGICAL GIRLS TELL ALL
FALL FASHI
IT'S OUT!

OF COURSE THEY PUT MIA ON THE COVER.
LUSH PARFUM

THIS AIN'T A LIBRARY, MA'AM.
SORRY...
BIG OL MUSCLE MAG
CARROT ALL

WHAT!?

the Golden Era Girls

where are they Now?

FIND OUT!

LILY HEINS

JAYDA WELLS

What was it like?

"WE LOOKED CUTE AND HAD SOME FUN!"

JENNY S.

The Glamorous Lifestyles of former Magical-Girls!

"... WE LOOKED CUTE AND HAD SOME FUN."
- Former Teen Troop 5 member.
THEY DIDN'T EVEN USE MY NAME!
WHAT'S GOING ON?
DID YOU JUST WAKE UP!?
AND I WOULDA KEPT SLEEPING IF YOU WEREN'T OUT HERE YELLING!!
IT'S HALF PAST NOON.
IT'S SATURDAY.
SO WHY ARE YOU OUT HERE YELLING AT A MAGAZINE ON A SATURDAY MORNING?
AFTERNOON.
WHO CARES?

REMEMBER THE INTERVIEW I DID WITH GIRL GIRL MAGAZINE LAST MONTH?

NO.

WELL, THEY COMPLETELY QUOTED ME OUT OF CONTEXT. AND THEY DIDN'T EVEN USE MY NAME.

AND THEN WHAT?

BLUSH PARFUM

CEREAL PUFFS

I GOTTA GO SEE NIKKI TODAY.
SHE JUST BROKE UP WITH BRENT AND STEPH IS BEING A BITCH.
LAZY GIRL
Beauty Hacks

HEY! WATCH IT!
GIRLS NEED TO SUPPORT EACH OTHER.

NOT MY FAULT STEPH'S BEING BITCHY.

SEE YA!
ARE YOU GOING OUT LIKE THAT?
YEAH, MOM. WHO CARES?

SLAM

CEREAL PUFF

CEREAL PUFFS
NEW

TEEN TROOP S

BLOG ZONE
SIGN IN:
USERNAME:
PASSWORD:
OR Sign up!
FORGOT PASSWORD?

I DON'T TAKE MANY INTERVIEWS THESE DAYS. MAINLY BECAUSE NOBODY ASKS BUT ALSO BECAUSE THE MEDIA REFUSES TO DISCUSS THE TRUTH ABOUT THE MAGICAL GIRL-INDUSTRIAL COMPLEX.

AND THAT'S WHY I BLOG.

BUT IT ALSO MAKES ME NERVOUS BECAUSE SHE'S A RECKLESS TEEN AND WHO KNOWS WHAT SHE'LL END UP SPENDING HER OWN MONEY ON...

COSMIC CULT. #5 VOL 2

FLOWER ALLIGATOR

COSMIC CULT # 6

VOL. 2

FLOWER ALLIGATOR

COSMIC CULT 7

VOL 2

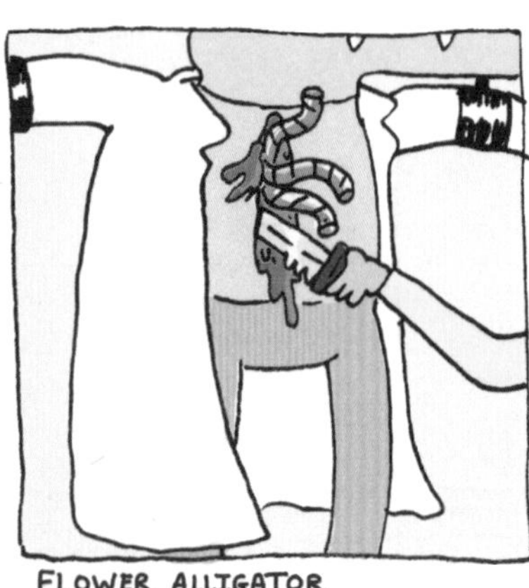

FLOWER ALLIGATOR

SWAMPLORD

FLOWER ALLIGATOR

FLOWER ALLIGATOR

SWAMPLORD

BEDSIDE MANNERS
ALL AILMENTS WELCOME
bark!
vvrrroooooom!

MOTIVATION
NOD
OK.
I'M TAKING YOUR HOLO AND YOU CAN GO THROUGH THAT DOOR
HELLO?
MMMM
COME IN...
M D
TAKE A SEAT.
I'M A DR
PILLS AND SUCH
WELCOME, PATIENT SCUM!

I'M DOCTOR DOCTOR
NOW, WHO MIGHT YOU BE?
MY NAME'S PIXIE
I'VE BEEN HAVING A PROBLEM W/ MY HAND- WELL, MY WHOLE ARM. I PUT IT OFF FOR TOO LONG AND YOU WERE THE ONLY DOCTOR THAT WOULD SEE ME ON SUCH SHORT NOTICE
UH-HUH
BY THE LOCKERS SEASON 8
HEHE
THIS IS HOW THINGS HAVE UNFOLDENDED:
I'VE BEEN SLEEPING ON MY ARM A LOT
I SLEEP W/ EARBUDS, SO I COULDN'T HAVE HEARD IT WAILING
I OFTEN WAKE UP W/ PINS AND NEEDLES
A WEEK AGO, IT LOST ALL SENSATION,
LEAVING ME W/ A LIMP ARM NOODLE.
DRAGGING IT AROUND HAS BECOME SUCH A NUISANCE
OH MY, HOW UNFORTUNATE
I. AM. GOD.
bump
whisper
OOOHH... HEHEHE
MY SOURCES HAVE COME UP WITH JUST THE UNGUENT FOR YOU

THANK YOU, DOCTOR!!!
sniff
PLEASE, CALL ME DOCTOCTOR.
AND YOU'RE WELCOME, KID
slap slap
DING-DONG! LUNCHTIME = TIME TO GIT
UH... OKAY.
I'M A DR
bobble
WHEN SHOULD I EXPECT RESULTS?
LET'S SEE...
I'VE GOT LIKE 7 SEASONS LEFT AND I LIKE TO BE A RUMINANT WATCHER... LET'S SAY FOUR MONTHS
UGH... NO PAPRIKA
UM--
SERVICED SCUM USE THE SLIDE
THE SAGA SLIDE
OH GOD!
EXIT
FORGOT YOUR PRESCRIPTION, BOYYY
chomp
retch
?

OH HOW TIME PASSES BY
DESERT DRY
STILL RIP
A
B
SSSS
4 MONTHS LATER!
TIME'S UP!
DOCTOCTOR!
typing
typing
PLEASE GO THROUGH THE DOOR, SIR
IT'S BEEN FOUR WHOLE MONTHS!
ooohhh...
OI!
crack!
GRRR
I'VE EVEN HIT PUBERTY!
I HAVE TO FUCKING WEAR CLOTHES NOW!

WHAT ARE YOU GOING TO DO ABOUT THIS ?
YIKES! HOW FIERCE! OH, TO BE YOUNG
IS THAT WHY YOU WATCH TEEN DRAMAS ALL DAY?
IT'S A DECONSTRUCTION! HOW DARE YOU!
LISTEN, THESE ARE TRYING TIMES. LAYOFFS AND WHATNOT
GRRRRRRRR
I'M FILLING IN FOR EVERY PERSON IN THE BUILDING
I DON'T CARE!
NO MORE UNGUENTS
RESULTS!
MY BUD HAS BLOOMED
I DON'T KNOW IF YOU'VE NOTICED...
SO WHAT?
IT'S NICE, I GUESS?
IT HAS TAKEN A LIKING TO
YOUR FEISTGEIST, BOY
whisper
whisper
MMM...! WHAT A BRIGHT IDEA! WITH MY POWER AS A STAND-IN HYPNOTIST, I WILL DEAL WITH THIS ONCE AND FOR ALL.
HUH?
SCHLEP.
thump

-CAN YOU HEAR ME?
-YES
-ahem... A FUTURE IS LOOMING AHEAD. IT IS NECESSARY THAT YOU ADAPT TO POSSIBILITY.
-YES
-YOUR ARM SEPARATES AND BUILDS A LIFE OF ITS OWN
TELL ME ABOUT THAT FUTURE, BOY!
MY ARM... WOULD VEER OFF CONFUSED BUT SLOWLY BUILD CONFIDENCE
IT WOULD EVENTUALLY LEARN HOW TO INTERACT WITH ITS ENVIRONMENT!
IT WOULD GET A JOB AS A WEALTH MANAGEMENT ADVISOR
IT WOULD GO ON EXPLORATION TRAVELS
BINGE SHOUNEN
TAKE UP AN INSTRUMENT
DISCOVER TREASURE
FALL IN LOVE
LOVE
RAISE NON-BIOLOGICAL CHILDREN
LEARN A SECOND AND THIRD LANGUAGE
FEEL CONTENT EVERY NOW AND THEN
-WONDERFUL...

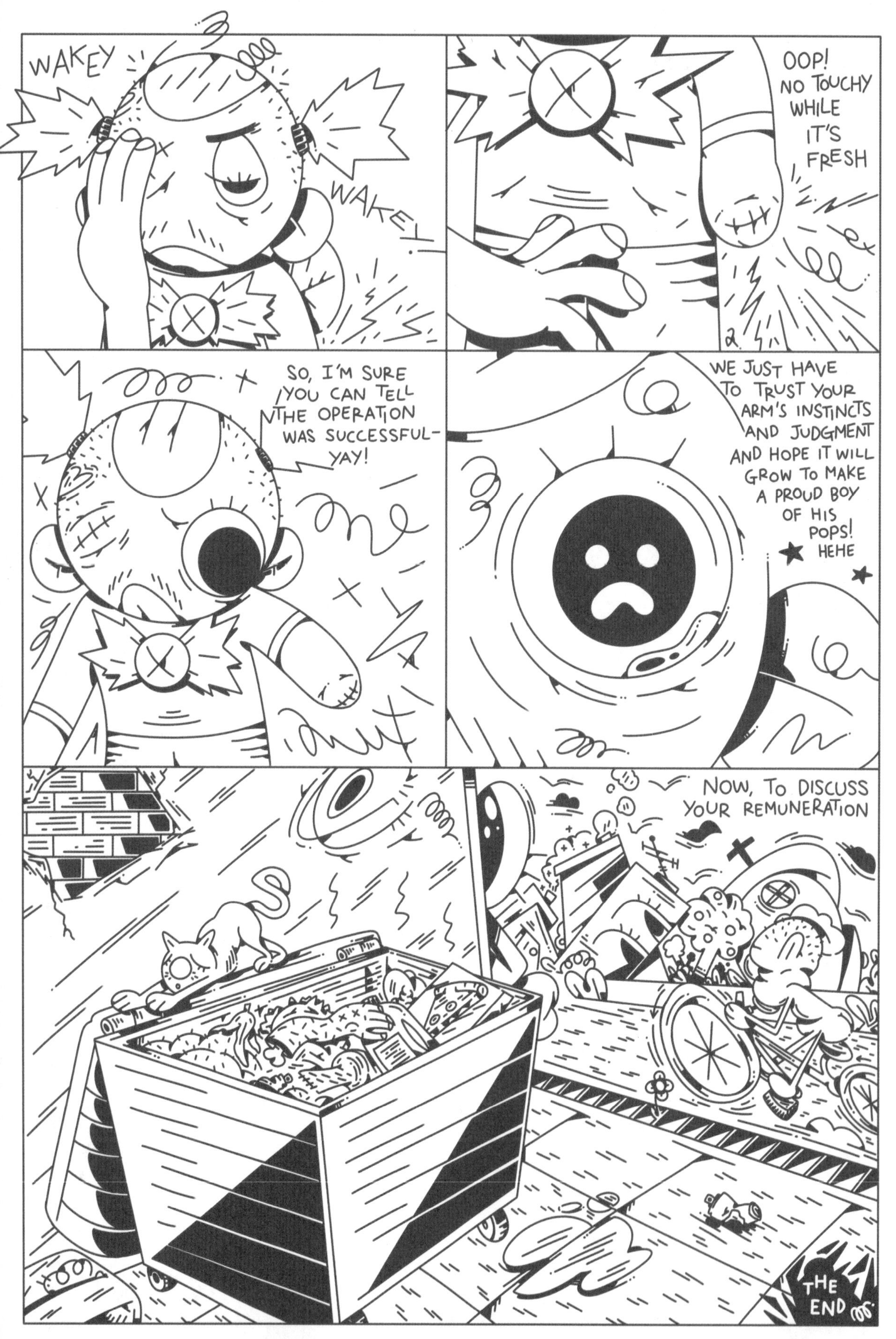
WAKEY
WAKEY!
OOP! NO TOUCHY WHILE IT'S FRESH
SO, I'M SURE YOU CAN TELL THE OPERATION WAS SUCCESSFUL-YAY!
WE JUST HAVE TO TRUST YOUR ARM'S INSTINCTS AND JUDGMENT AND HOPE IT WILL GROW TO MAKE A PROUD BOY OF HIS POPS! HEHE
NOW, TO DISCUSS YOUR REMUNERATION
THE END

CATS and FROGS

WHEN ANGELS SPLASHED ABOUT THIS POND - THEN SURELY WAS I BORN

YET MOMENTS COME WHEN POOLS TURN BLOOD -

THE BREATH OF DEATH IS WARM!

!

WHAT MONSTROUS HEAD! UNNERVING EYES!

AND EARS LIKE DEVIL'S WINGS!

THE MOON, ALOOF, CASTS CRYPTIC LIGHT ON US FOUR - FOOTED THINGS

D.RINYLO

CATS *and* FROGS

A CAT DOESN'T WALK – IT SLINKS...

THEY DON'T REALLY DO MUCH BUT BLINK

SNIFF

LUDICROUS BEAST!

THEY'RE FLUFFY, AT LEAST!

SCREW YOU GUYS – I'M JUST GETTING A DRINK

D.RINYLO

CATS and FROGS

THERE'S A GREAT WIDE CRAZY WORLD OUTSIDE

D.RINYLO

WITH BIG TALL FUCKING TREES

CLIMB THEM WITH YOUR EYES, AT LEAST!

GET OFF THOSE LITTLE SCREENS!

HOP DUDE

BY DAVE MERCIER

ALIVE

POWER

NEWS

ZEN

BABY

MODERATION

OOPS

POISON FLOWERS
& PANDEMONIUM
A Richard Sala Omnibus

STONE FRUIT
LEE LAI

THE INTERNET URBAN LEGEND IS TRUE!
RED ROOM
BY ED PISKOR
See— MURDER ON THE DARK WEB. FOR FUN AND PROFIT!
See— RIVERS OF GORE!
See— ILLEGAL ACTS OF CARNOGRAPHY AND DEGRADATION, LIVE ON WEBCAM!
FIRST ISSUE!

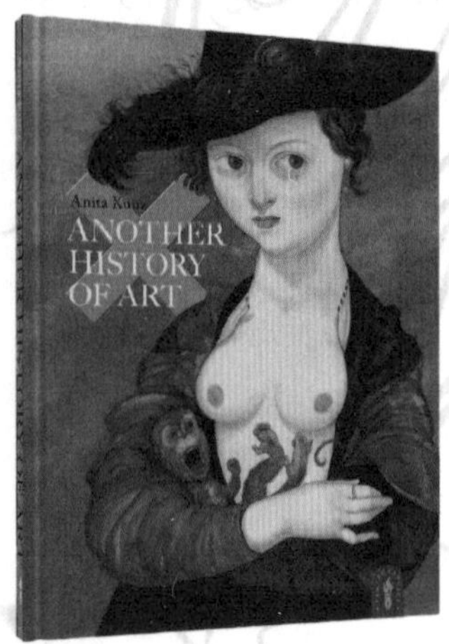
Anita Kunz
ANOTHER HISTORY OF ART

NATHAN COWDRY'S
CRASH SITE

ZIG ZAG

THE FUTURE IS FEMALE

Chartwell Manor
A Comics Memoir by GLENN HEAD
"This is—well, okay, I'll say it: A MASTERPIECE! Truly" —R. CRUMB

BARRY WINDSOR-SMITH
MONSTERS

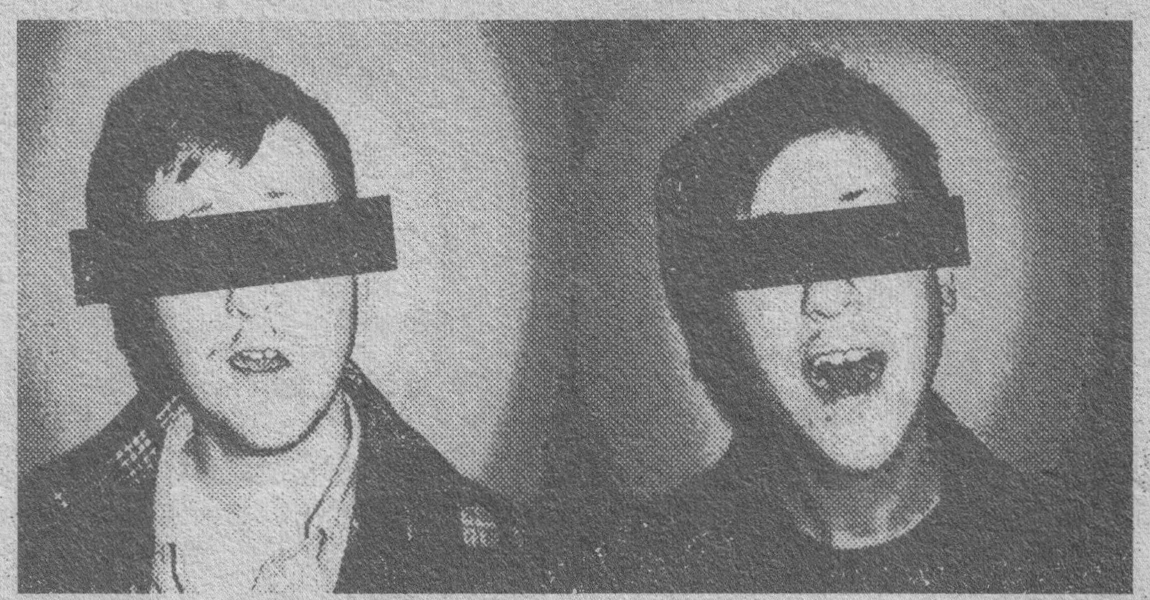

Johnny Pemberton

Prank Call Masterclass

Johnny Pemberton is the host of the strange and surreal podcast "Live to Tape," they have a cassette tape of prank calls through Starburns Industries called "Recorded for Quality Assurance," do stand up comedy, and can be seen in movies and television shows.

We spoke to them about their history with prank calling and picked up some of their techniques and philosophy.

GB: All right. So what I want to start with is, what's the first prank call you remember making?

JP: Ah, man. The first prank call I remember making is probably, I know I did ones before this, but the first one I actually really remember was with this guy. A friend of my dad's or some coworker of his who was visiting from Canada and he brought his son with him. He was about my age, maybe a year or two older or younger. And we called some people because he was into prank phone calls.

We were staying at his house or something. We were kind of forced to be friends. I remember we did some really basic prank phone calls with him claiming to be the name Johnny Combat. Doing kinda like a Canadian accent. "Heyyy," I can't even do it, but "Johnny Combat" like in a weird Canadian accent. I just remember doing that because I think we tried to record them. I don't know if I did or not, but I just remember doing that with him. For some reason I can definitely remember that.

GB: So prank calls are something you've always done?

JP: Yeah. It's something I've been doing for a long time. I can't think how I first heard about it. Maybe it was the Jerky Boys, but maybe it wasn't.

GB: Did you own any of the Jerky Boys CDs?

JP: I had one of the Jerky Boys albums. I wasn't like, I didn't love it. I thought it was pretty cool. What got me really into this stuff was Longmont Potion Castle when I heard them.

That really got me into stuff and just sort of realizing what you could do with it. But I suppose I was doing a lot before that and I just liked, I don't know, something about it. I just liked doing it.

I think what I like to do is to make people laugh who are listening to me do a live call. I think I heard about someone's brother or something like that doing a call where he would find someone's name in the phone book and call them up and pretend like they know them. I did that once to some people and I couldn't believe it actually worked. And how well it worked. 'Cause I was super nice.

GB: Have you heard the Jerry Lewis calls? There's a bunch of like Jerry Lewis prank calls.

JP: Like the actor?

GB: Yeah, from like the sixties. They are ancient. He didn't have like, a great style. He basically just annoyed people, but apparently when he was in the dressing room he would just call people to kill time.

JP: That's funny. I guess that makes sense. I can see him doing that. I felt like he's, uh, I dunno. I like a lot of the stuff that he did and that seems like, I'm not surprised that he did that. (laughing)

GB: Have you listened to the Jerky Boys stuff more recently?

JP: I haven't. No.

GB: I recently went back and listened to it. It's absurdly mean and offensive.

JP: It is. Yeah. I remember that being the case. It's interesting. I read an article about him recently. I thought what was cool was that he used to call from complete darkness.

He would make the phone call in the completely dark room. And I think about that and that's such a good idea cause it's like this thing where there's nothing there. You're just drawing from what's in your head. And I've done some stuff recently in total darkness and just found it to be the most fun. I mean, just the greatest experience. It's like so psychedelic with no psychedelics.

GB: So you've been doing a lot of calls more recently and phone books aren't really a thing anymore.

JP: Right.

GB: So you can pretty much only call businesses and know who you're going to talk to, or somebody you know.

JP: Pretty much. Yeah.

GB: Has that affected the way you choose who you call?

JP: It did for me. That's what started the whole new thing of making calls was because of that. Because when I started doing prank calls from my old podcast, "Twisting the Wind," I would do it to businesses because businesses that are taking calls in have to record them for "quality assurance." And so if they're recording it, that's sort of a loophole.

I mean supposedly it's a loophole. I don't know if it's held up in court or anything, but it's this thing where they're recording it so you can record it.

GB: Because of two-party consent?

JP: Yeah, it's two-party consent, because if they're saying we're recording it, that means that they're also acknowledging the fact that they are being recorded themselves. So it gives you license to record it without asking them permission to record it.

GB: That makes sense.

JP: That's what someone told me who used to work on Crank Yankers. And I um, I just took that was like, OK, well I'm just going to run with that and if I get sued or cease and desist, that would be awesome. But it hasn't happened and I doubt it will.

GB: When you're deciding to call somebody, do you tend to gravitate toward things that you have had experiences with or places you've been, or do you just go with something you've never had any contact with?

JP: I like to do definitely something that I have a reason to talk to someone about. That's nice.

I do like to do it to certain places. I used to make a lot of calls to Oklahoma because I felt like that was this weird window of politeness and also sort of laziness, where they have time to talk. I think people in the South are just more willing to talk to people, to weirdos, and not get pissed off. More just allow their time to be wasted.

And a lot of it was places that were like big. Places like Walmart. I used to call like individual Walmarts in small places in the Midwest. Just because I felt like that was like so faceless and such a big thing. You could probably get away with more. It's also like kind of like fishing because it's like a bigger lake. So there's maybe more of a likelihood there will be a fish that you can reel in for a long time.

GB: So when you're making a call, how much of the bit do you have in mind generally before you start? Do you like to just go in with nothing and just, you know...

JP: Yeah, usually I go in with nothing. A lot of times what I think about is I want to find out what someone had for lunch. I want to find out something sort of personal. Like, where in the world they are, the weather. If it's tangential to the product or something, I will try to ask sort of experience-based questions about the product that I think maybe they won't be able to answer. That's usually about as much as I go in with.

I guess it's always about where I'm calling from — calling like the bakery of a grocery store, I want to ask about having a cake made.It's the shape of a sphere or something like that.

Like a thing that I usually try to think about is: What's the most absurd thing I could ask for? And also, what's the nicest way to ask for that absurd thing and try to get people to help me with their own personal opinions and how they think about the thing I'm asking about. I think that's the big thing.

I called Aveda once, the haircare company, and I was talking to this girl. She wasn't very interested, but then I mentioned something about what she thought about the product and she just lit up and start talking about her hair and stuff.

And it really worked because that way I could sort of just keep asking her stuff because she was talking about herself, and everyone likes talking about themselves. I mean, not everyone, but like the one in three people who work with customer service, you can trick them into talking about themselves because they think they're helping you by doing that, which a lot of times they are. So I guess it's that.

That was that the question I guess? I don't know.

GB: Yeah, I think that was good!

Yeah. So how do you feel about calling the same people back? What are your feelings about that?

JP: Um, I haven't really done it except for a few times. I don't really like it 'cause I feel like it's just sort of, uh, it starts to become a relationship.

And if it's something where I'm not being fully truthful about something, I kind of feel... I guess I don't feel bad so much as I just feel like I'm not as interested in that because the novelty is gone. Like in terms of calling someone back.

GB: I do feel like one of the reasons I like your stuff and Longmont Potion Castle is you guys are never explicitly mean to people. Like very often.

JP: Sometimes those guys can be pretty fucking mean. I don't have the balls they do. I don't. I get scared when I get into some sort of confrontation like that, but they just like double down. But I feel like they're good at doubling down in the sense where they make it be like "Oh, it's absurd you're getting angry."

GB: Yeah. They mostly do it like when somebody gets angry, angry at something that's inappropriate to be angry about. That seems to be where they really double down, unlike the Jerky Boys where they just call and start yelling at people.

JP: Right. Yeah. I guess I don't really like being mean because I feel like... I just don't enjoy it as much, 'cause I don't think it's as funny and I just feel like you can get so much

more stuff if you basically let a person be the one who makes a fool of themself or the opposite. You end up finding something to talk to them about.

You would have no idea that you'd be talking to someone you don't know about something so intimate, or you know, not intimate. But um, but just sort of a, like there's a mutual, there's like a connection, an actual connection that happens.

GB: If you're comfortable saying, on your call on your cassette "Recorded for Quality Assurance," you call a strip club called Show & Tel.

JP: Oh, I do. I didn't, I didn't think I said it in the call but you figured it out.

GB: They kind of say it. You ask if there's just one L in the name. Is that the Show & Tel Philadelphia?

JP: Yes it is.

GB: Are you comfortable with me putting that down?

JP: I don't mind saying that 'cause it, I mean it's like what, what's going to happen?

GB: Nothing, but like I feel like somebody who sees it might then continue on your bit or something and that can just be annoying.

JP: I think that that was a lightning strike and it's in the extreme. That was a pure lightning strike. That will never happen again.

That's something where that was so lucky and just weird and strange and that guy happened to, to bother to answer all my questions that way. That like a weird, weird one. Yeah.

That was something too where I called my friend Brendan who was from Philadelphia. He gave me a bunch of numbers and I didn't know what I was calling. I called the cops, the police station, not knowing I was calling a police station, and that was a cool one. I called them twice, and same with Show & Tel. I didn't know what I was calling.

GB: Well and then on that track, like he answers so many questions for so long. Why do you think people stay on the phone for so long? Like past the point where they're obviously being fucked with?

JP: Well I think a lot of people don't think they're being fucked with because people are so strange.

There's no, there's no end to the amount of real people who ask the dumbest, most absurd things who are also extremely lonely and will call Crate and Barrel at three o'clock in the morning and talk to someone for as long as they possibly can.

I know there are a bunch of people I think who probably masturbate on the phone in a way that's like not very erotic but they're still doing it. So there's just all kinds of weird shit that goes on in the customer service phone world to where I think if you play it right, if I was one of the ones you heard, where I have played it right, there are obviously tons of them to get hang ups or people are just like, they know something's up.

But if you play it right to the right person, they don't think something's up.

And also, uh, the big thing is that they're not allowed to hang up. If you're calling a customer service line and you're not being abusive or using any bad words and you're talking about the product or whatever it is you're doing, they can't hang up. I talked to some girl in Malaysia for like two-and-a-half hours once.

So it's just because they, they can't hang up.

And also I used to work in calls. The thing is if you're working in a call center, when you're on the phone, time goes five times faster than when you're either making calls, or waiting to get them.

So it's, people enjoy talking on the phone more than anything else. And it's because you don't get, unless it's like a survey thing, you don't get paid per completion.

You're there, you're there to answer calls and if you're on the phone it's so much more engaging.

And your day is better. And so if I can like feather that line and keep them on the phone, I think that's good for people. Also a lot of times I think people do know they're being fucked with, but they like it. Yeah. They like it especially if it's something they're not being fucked with in a mean way. They're just sort of being this person.

It's spinning a yarn.

GB: Yeah. Cool. Yeah. Thank you.

JP: Thanks a lot man.

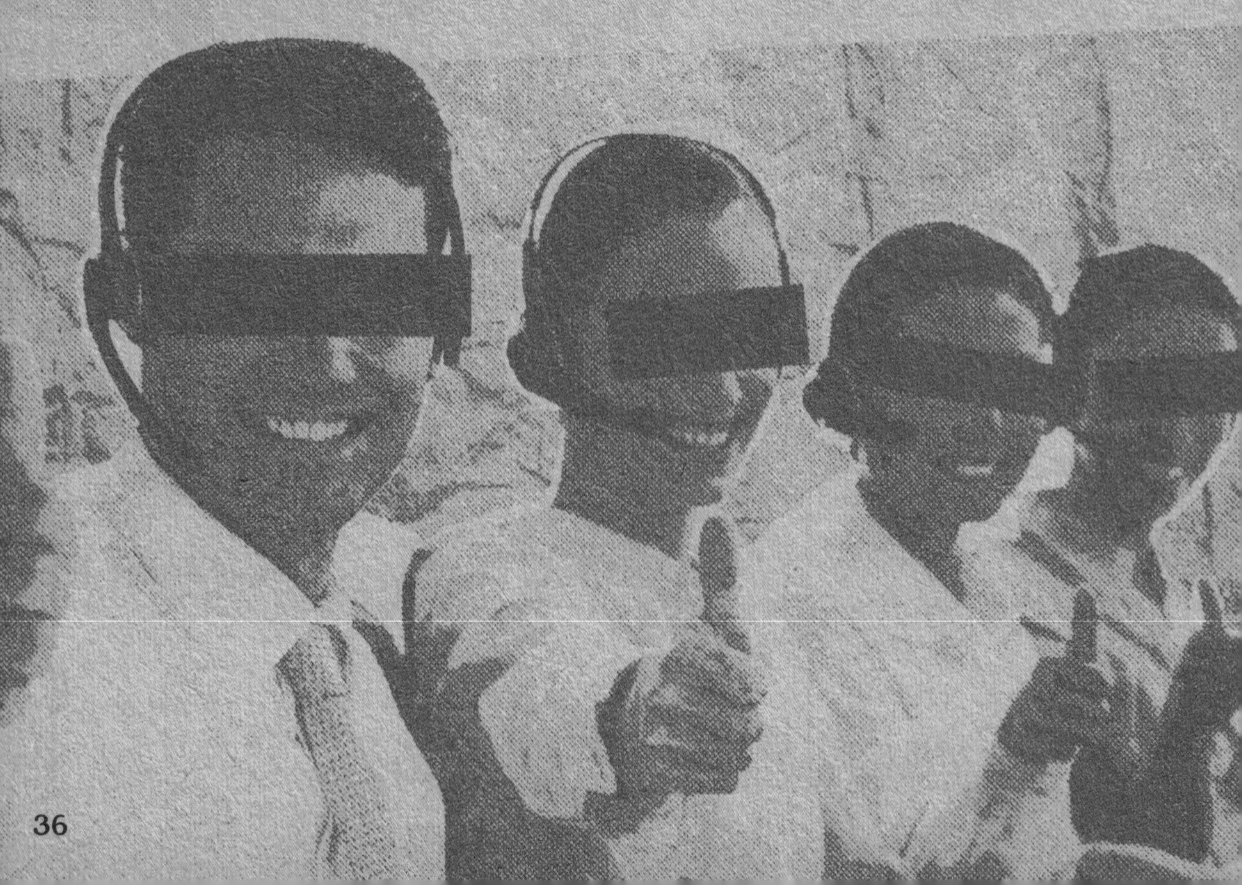

EGGCREAM

Welcome To Pacific City always in motion
14 FT 1 IN
Mam, please sit down. I'm not going to ask you again.
And I'm not going to ask you again to not use that tone of voice with me.

Can you believe the attitude on that driver?
Unbelievable.

I'm just glad we made it here in one piece. That driver was a maniac.
CASINO
CASINO
We're blessed.

I need to find a change machine and a bathroom pronto.
Never prepared. I have change. I'll be playing at the machines.
I'll come find you when I'm done.
Here we go...
Excuse me miss, would you like a drink?
Oh! Don't EVER scare me like that! You almost gave Gruffles a heart attack!
I'm sorry miss.
Now we're all shook up! If I drop dead your casino will have a major lawsuit on it's hands!
Miss I'm sorry! Let me comp you at the buffet.
I guess that'll do.
Now I'm too nervous to play. Come on Gruffles let's find Hazel.
And I'll take a gin and tonic!
CHING!

What are you doing sitting around? Let's go to the buffet.
Thank God. I'm woozy from the long drive.

Oh, no. Look at this line. Nuh-uh.

Excuse me pardon me excuse me...
Excuse me pardon me
what the-

We're comp'd for this meal. We're not waiting in line. And I suggest you call your supervisor if you have a problem with that.
EXIT

Look at this lousy food...
Feh!

Awful, Mmm...
Terrible.

Let me tell you something- if this meal wasn't comp'd I'd request a refund.
Oh, absolutely.
Let's grab something for the road and get outta here.

ESCALATOR
EXIT
Oh boy, I'm stuffed. Let's walk outside for a little bit.

CASINO
DICE
SAND CASINO

Let's sit down. It's so crowded here.

Look at these low lives.

SPLAT!

OH MY GOD! A BIRD SHIT ON ME!

Relax. It's good luck.

SPLAT!

EW THERE'S SHIT ALL OVER ME THAT'S DISGUSTING!

Hurry up - this is an ambush!
Cover your head! I hear more birds!
FRESH
NEW

I think I've had enough luck today.

Don't say such a thing! We haven't even played yet!

Oh yeah.
Let's sit down.

Do you have a coin I can use?
Why?

I wanna throw one in the fountain for good luck before we start.

'Scuse me!
whoa!

CLINK!

We're leaving right now! This casino is bad energy!
Oh, please...

Whoops!
ARF!

Oh my God! Gruffles! There's bad energy here! We're leaving!
Sorry.

I have a very good sense of energy and this place is very bad.

So... same time next weekend?
yah
CASINO
END!?

by Bastian Najdek // getxxlost

SOMEWHERE IN THE EAST GALAXY...

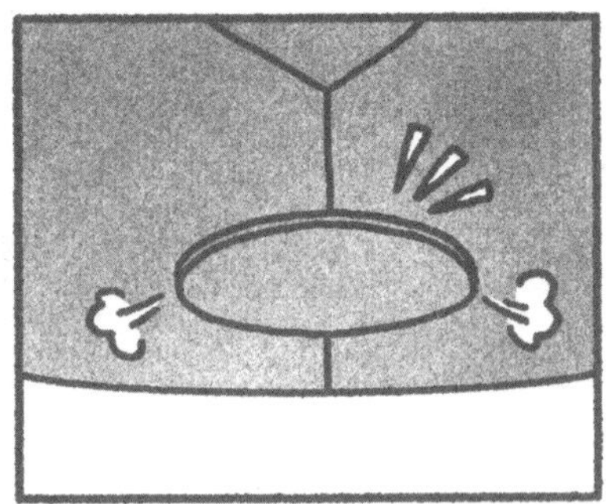

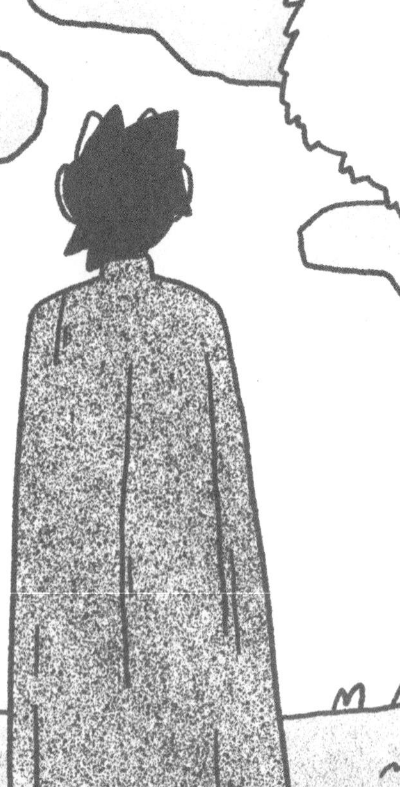

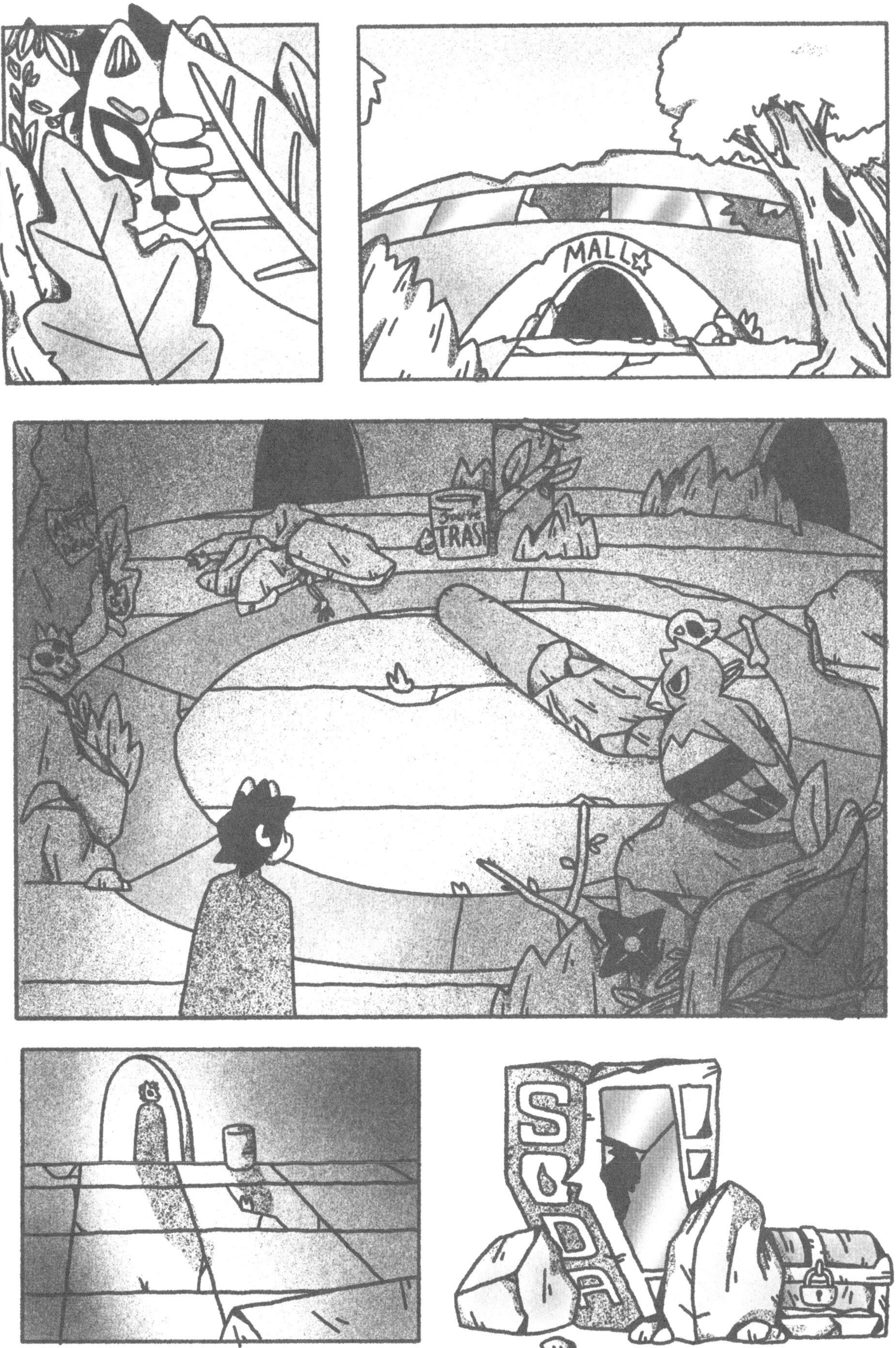

MALL

SODA

ゾクッ
SFX: SHIVER
!?
TO BE CONTINUED??? 0_0

MEGACOSM

EPISODE 1

By Steve Thueson

BOOM!

They've broken through the east wall!

They've opened fire!

We can't ho-*kssssssss*

We've lost, captain! We have to plan an escape

We can't afford to let Beni fall into their hands

Don't worry, I won't let them take you

Are there any ships available?

Negative, Captain! All ships have been destroyed!

I'm gonna make a call...

...Let's hope
somebody answers

This suuuuucks!

Hey, don't blame me!
What's that supposed to mean?

I'm just saying, it would've been nice if you hadn't missed so many credit payments

Cause maybe then we wouldn't have bounty hunters after us all the time
That's not fair!

With how little I make doing transports, and all the maintenance this ship needs for the transports, I barely have enough for food, let alone credit payments

Ok...

But you keep buying all these movies

It's called Self Care, Ok?!

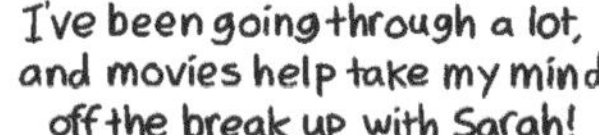

Well, this ship should be able to get up to light speed, we can try that to get outta here and make it to the pick up location

I have you now

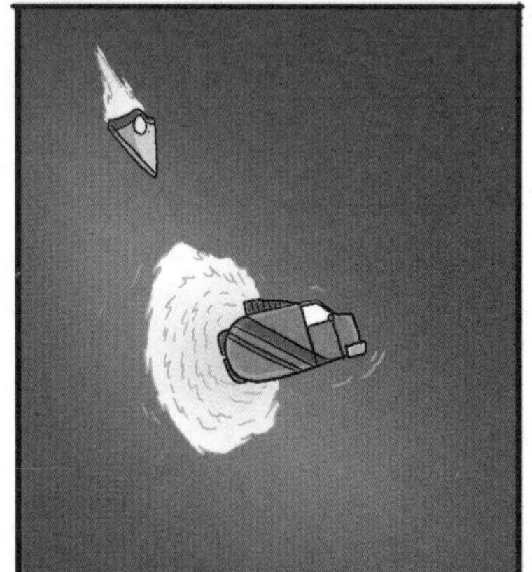

NO!
WRR WRR WRR
WRR WRR WRR
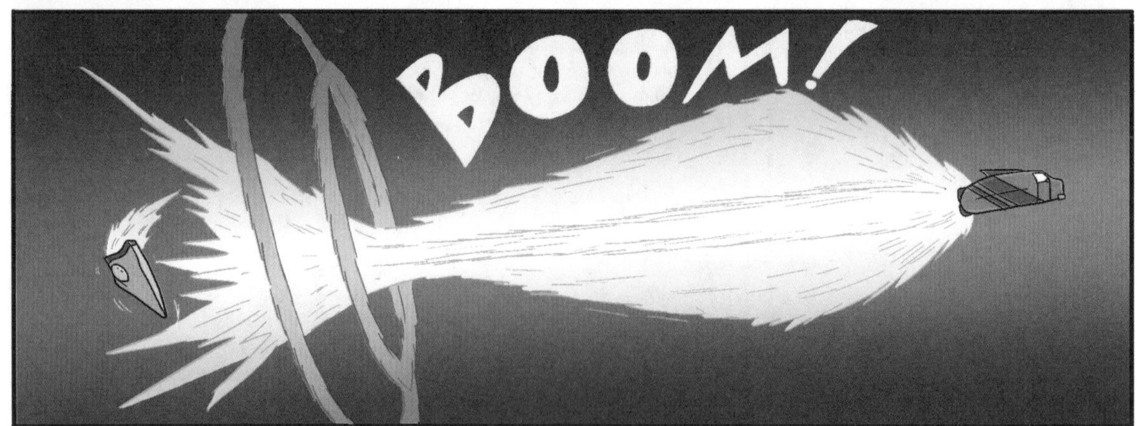
BOOM!

You can't run forever, Jake!

I'll find you

Man, this
place is wrecked

I can't even see
anyone down there
Do they
know we're here?

I've been trying
to reach them, but no
one's responded

You're gonna have
to go down there
and find them

But it's on fire!
Well, somebody
has to go down there!

And I'm attached
to the ship!

FINE!

Well I hope you
have fun sitting in
here all day!
Hopefully when I die
from fire you won't
have to get up!
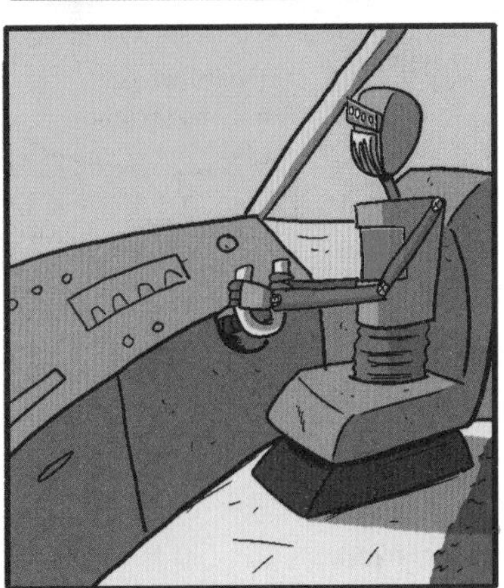

Hey, dude, I'm
sorry, that was mean
I'm just
scared of fire

The call came from this platform, see if you can find anyone who looks like they'd need a transport

Do... uh...
do you, uh...

Do you want
some gum?
What?

I don't know, I'm
just trying to help
With
gum?

I mean, yeah? Gum is
fun, it'll take your mind off...
... off
of things?

Gum's not fun
Well not, like,
fun fun
But I like
to chew gum!
Do you not like
to chew gum?
Well...

Oh geeze, wait, I'm making
this all about me! Forget it!
I'm sorry, you don't need
to want gum
No, hey,
come on

I'd love
some gum

What is this?
Mint?
Yeah.
You don't like it

No, no

It's good

You wouldn't happen to know anyone looking for a transport outta here?

Well, if it's the captain she'll be somewhere in there

But be careful

You'll be in grave danger

Hmmm...

"grave danger"
Freakin' liar

Hello?!

Anyone in there call for a transport?!

Schooom

Y'all order a transport?
Quick, get in!

No, no the ship's waiting outsi–

GAAAH!

It's an ambush!

What is happening?!

I'm getting us out of here

Now hand me that grenade

BOOOM

Let's go let's go!

You said the transport was parked outside, right?

guh...

uh...

uh...

uh...

Lord Zarth has been expanding his reach over the galaxy

As each system falls under his control, his power seems only to grow

But even he understands that this power is finite

Zarth seeks to create a weapon capable of piercing the very Cosmos itself
Thus unlocking its limitless potential and becoming more powerful than anyone could imagine

The only one with the knowledge to accomplish such a feat is the famed scientist Beni

The key to Zarth's weapon lies in Beni's mind
And Zarth will stop at nothing to get it

Which is why it's imperative that we get Beni out of danger and into safe hands

What?

Dude, are you even listening to me?
Yeah yeah
The guy's after the guy

I just wasn't expecting to run so much
I wasn't even expecting to take this job, but I'm way behind on credit payments

I mean, everybody gets behind on stuff like that sometimes
That's what I've been saying!

Lots of people forget to pay their bills for two or three years!
Who cares?!

So how far is your ship?

It's hovering just outside

GAAAH!

You got any more grenades?

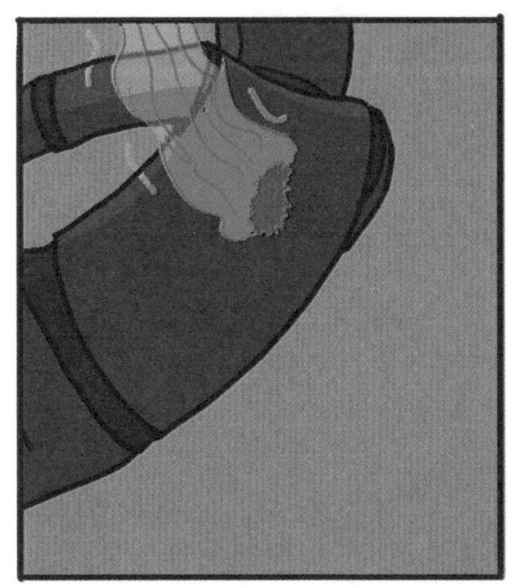

Ha! Yes!

No!

This guy's been after me all day!

Go! Go! Go!

Come on!
Come on!
Alright buddy, that's all of 'em, let's go!
Oh geeze
Oh geeze
Oh geeze
Oh geeze
gasp!
Mint Gum!
You're all clear kid, now pick me up and let's—
oh

Well alright!

Looks like it's just a quick trip to your destination and then you'll be good to go!

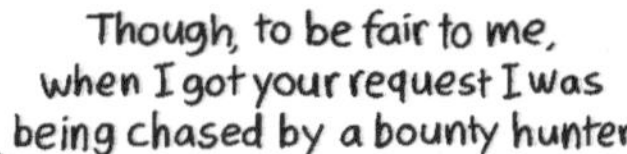

I'm so glad you made it here safely

When I heard of the attack I was so worried

But seeing you all here, together, gives me hope that we can turn the tide in this war

Now, let us plan our next move, we may have this small victory, but we still need all the help we can get

Hey, Wait!

I think I left my phone in the ship, can I look around real quick?

oh, yeah... of course

Thanks!

Okay, got it! Thanks for the ride Jim!

You okay, bud?

Yeah, I guess
I get it

It can be tricky being around people so fiercely devoted to a cause
To fighting injustice

It's inspiring, of course, but it can also make you feel like you're not doing enough
Even when you're doing all you can

Like you, you're... um...

You seem to be getting really into movies
Which is nice

Do you think they hate me?

I don't think they have any opinion on you
I feel like they were mad about the bed/couch thing

Well, yeah, your bed is gross
nobody wants to sit on something gross

You should clean up around here
Hey! I've been going through a lot!
Me and Sarah just—

This Suuuuucks!

To be continued...

GIRLS
GIRLS 
SOULMATES 
STRANGERS

LOVELESS
SOULMATES
STRANGERS

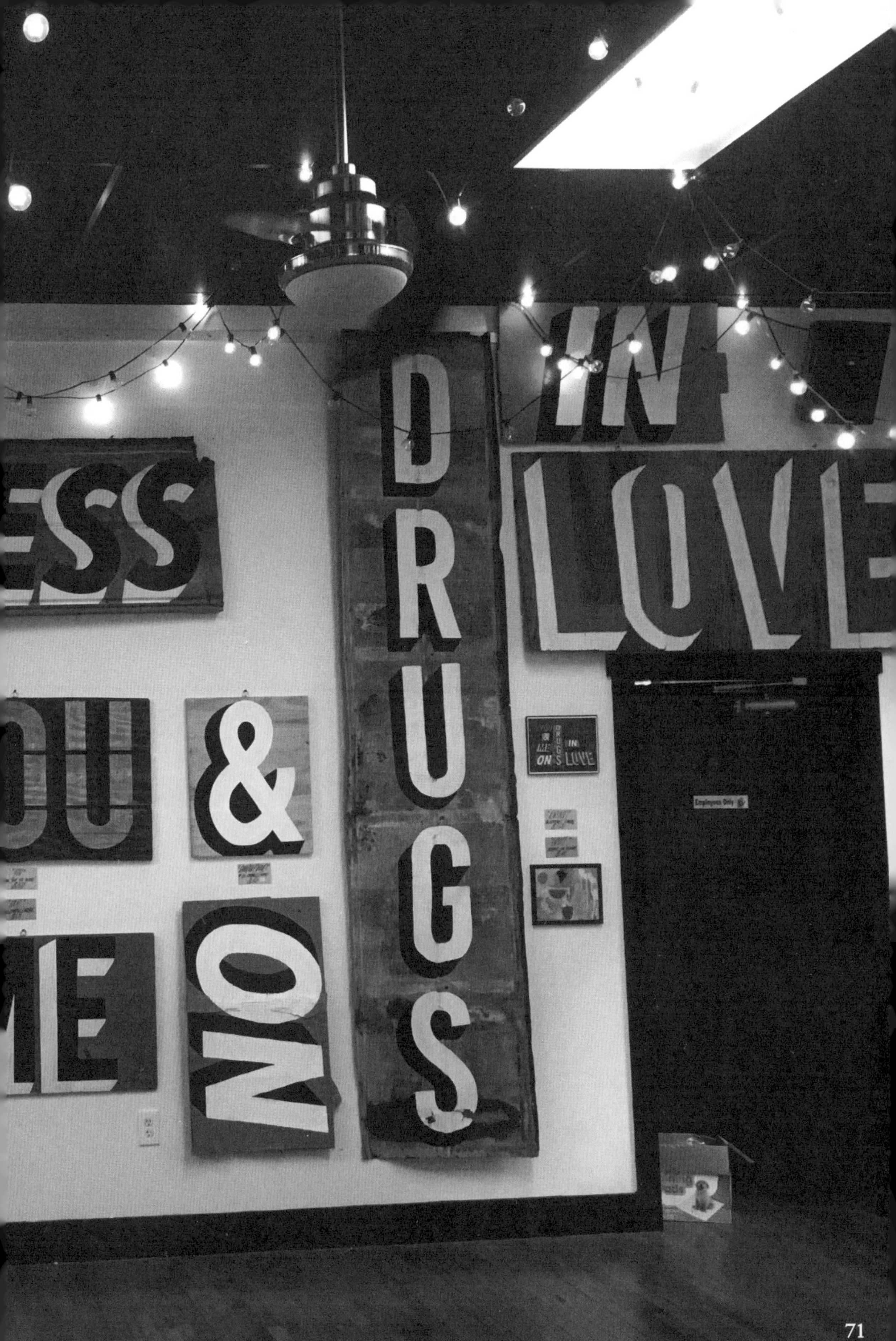
ESS
OU
&
DRUGS
IN
LOVE
Employees Only

CHILDRE

COME
BACK

HISS!

EVERYTHING SUCKS
SWEATER RULES!

GLUG!!!
BEER

PUFF!
CRUNCH!

COME ON MAN.
DON'T LITTER.

THIS IS A CEMETARY.
HAVE SOME RESPECT!
THE CRASS

I GOTTA HAND IT TO YA PHILLIPE.
YOU WERE RIGHT ABOUT THIS ONE.
THE CRASS
ZIP!

CAMPING IN THE CEMETARY BECAUSE IT'S TECHNICALLY ALSO A STATE PARK. HA!

IT'S ALMOST A PERFECT CRIME.

WOULD BE BETTER IF YOU BROUGH SOME REAL FOOD THOUGH...

ALRIGHT, CAMPING SUCKS.

DO YOU WANNA MAKE OUT OR SOMETHING?

COME ONNN...

MY PHONE IS DEAD.

WHAT?!

WHAT DID
I SAYYY?!
SLUMP!

WHY ARE
YOU SO
DRAMATIC?!

RIP

SSSSSS

RUSTLE RUSTLE!

GASP!

MOW.

SORRY I'M BEING WEIRD. I THINK I'M DEPRESSED.

HOLY SHIT!
WHAT IS THAT?!

RIP
HARE
RIP
KAZAA

GASP!

RUN!
MOVE THAT GREEN ASS!

SLASH!
RIP
LIME
WIRE

DO YOU KNOW THAT GUY?!

IS THAT DUDE AN OLD SCHOOL SERIAL KILLER?
WITH THE MASK AND SHIT?!

WHAT?!

WHO EVEN DOES THAT ANYMORE?!

FUCK!
HE LOCKED OUR EXIT!

HE'S THE REAL THING!

PLEASE!
I'M NOT READY TO DIE!
I NEVER EVEN WATCHED THE WIRE!

I SAID I WOULD, BUT WHO WANTS TO WATCH A SHOW ABOUT COPS?

TRIP!
AND 1

SHIT!
!

WELL, THE WIRE IS AS MUCH A CRITIQUE OF THE POLICE AS IT IS AN ENDORSEMENT.

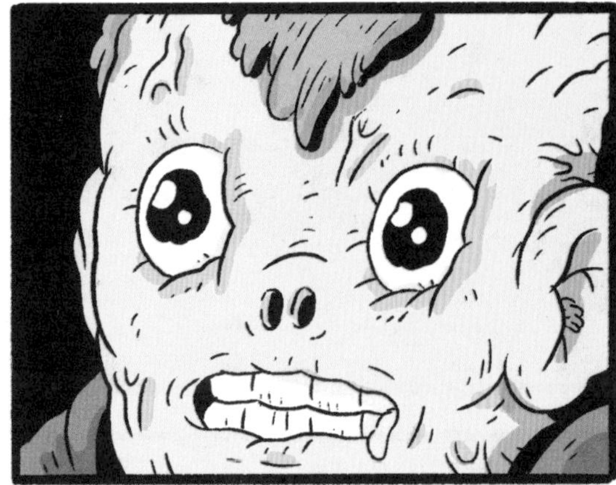

WHAT THE HECK?!

JUST BECAUSE I BROUGT YOU CAMPING AND TRIED TO KISS YOU DOESN'T MEAN WE ARE EXCLUSIVE OR ANYTHING...

ALSO, WE HAVE A LOT IN COMMON AND HE IS LIKE, REALLY PASSIONATE ABOUT HIS WORK AND SERIAL KILLER STUFF.
IT'S NOT LIKE I PLANNED ON THIS MAN.

WHATEVER.

SMOOCH!
KISS!
RUB RUB!
SMOOCH!

NO DUMPING!
A CATBOY OF MY VERY OWN

LAP
LAP
RUSTLE
RUSTLE
EAT SHIT
HISSSS
RATTLE
RATTLE
DAMN IT!

I STARTLED HIM AGAIN!
I WAS SO CLOSE!

I'VE BEEN WATCHING HIM FOR WEEKS.

WHEN I FIRST SAW HIM, I COULDNT BELIEVE MY LUCK!

A WILD CATBOY CROSSING MY PATH LIKE A DIVINE GIFT!

SINCE PUBERTY, I HAD LONGED FOR NOTHING ELSE...
CATBOY FANCY
LOVELESS
YAOI
INUYASHA

THAN
A CATBOY OF MY VERY OWN!

UGH!
FLEAS?!
YEAH, HE'S A LITTLE ROUGH AROUND THE EDGES,
SCRCH
SCRTCH

BUT WITH A BIT OF CLEANING UP AND SOME TRAINING...
OH BOY!
WILL YOU BE A GOOD BOY FOR ME?
DO YOU LIKE YOUR NEW OUTFIT?
YES, HE MUST BE MINE!

THIS OUGHT TO DO THE TRICK!
LOITERING
SNIFF SNIFF
MILK
AH!♡
HERE HE COMES!
EAT SHIT
OH YEAH! LAP IT UP♡
SNIFF
SWAT
AH!!
WHAT A WASTE!

I'M SURE HE'LL LIKE THESE.
OF COURSE HE WOULDN'T WANT MILK...
HE'S A GROWN CATBOY, NOT A KITTEN... HOW SILLY OF ME.
SARDINES
FANCY
I'M SURE SOON ENOUGH HE'LL BE BEGGING ME FOR MORE!
THANK YOU
RATTLE
OH! ALREADY? AREN'T YOU A HUNGRY BOY?
RATTLE
LICK
SCRAPE
SLURP
GET AWAY, YOU FOUL THING!!
THOSE ARE FOR MY CATBOY!!

WHAT AM I GOING TO DO?

SIGH
I JUST NEED TO FIND A WAY
TO GET CLOSE TO HIM.
POOP

WHAT TIME IS IT?
OH...
I THINK I MISSED WORK AGAIN...

WHATEVER. IT DOESNT MATTER. ALL THAT MATTERS IS -
SLURP

!!!
NOM
NOM

IT-IT'S YOU!

AND YOU REALLY SEEM TO LIKE PIZZA, HUH?

THIS IS IT! OUR MOMENT ♡ HAS ARRIVED! ♡ OH, ALL THE FUN WE'LL HAVE TOGETHER! ALL MY HOPES AND DREAMS!

Hmm?

OH, IS THIS WHAT YOU WANT NOW, NAUGHTY BOY?

GLUG
IS HE MINE NOW?
DO I DARE?

?
YES!

NOW, WHAT SHALL I CALL YOU, MY LOVELY LITTLE-

UGH!
NO!
?
NO!
NO!
YOU'RE DISGUSTING! GET AWAY FROM ME!
JEEZ. WHAT'S HIS PROBLEM?
WAHHH!
BUCK
PSSSS

HONEY, I'M HOME!

HEY!

WANT A BEER?
DUH! ALWAYS!
TRASH BABE

THEY'RE COURTESY OF THAT CREEPER I TOLD YOU ABOUT.
THE SAME ONE?

YEAH...
HEY, YOU WANNA MOVE THIS PARTY OVER TO TACO BELL?
MY TREAT.
HELL YEAH!

SO HE JUST GAVE YOU THE BEER?
YEAH, THEN I TOTALLY PISSED ON ALL HIS STUFF.
HA HA NOICE.
MAN, I'M GONNA GET LIKE 5 CRUNCH WRAPS!
GET AS MANY AS YOU WANT, BABE.
WE'RE LIVIN' IT UP TONIGHT!
THE END

dear Sparky

Charles "Sparky" Schulz was born in ----. He was named Sparky, after a cartoon horse. In an inspiring turn of events, he went on from being named after a cartoon horse to drawing Peanuts, the inspiration behind Snoopy shirts. We wanted to interview Sparky after learning of all of the trials he overcame to see what we could learn from him, but after kicking around the internet for a bit we found out he died.

Since we already publicly said we would interview him and had the space in the magazine set aside, we did the only thing we could do: We started contacting psychics on Facebook to see if we could organize a seance. The first surprise was to find out how many psychics there were in the middle of Arkansas. We were able to find five psychics through googling and were referred to one "paranormal investigator" by a tip on a local Facebook yard sale group.

The second surprise was how much integrity psychics have. Even in this economy, none of the psychics would meet with us even after offering a deposit ahead of time.

We did get some response from the head of our local "paranormal research society" chapter. After describing what we wanted, and them even explaining some of the tools they would use to measure whether we were in contact with the spirit of Mr. Schulz, they met with their board and told us that we were "messing around and not taking it seriously" and to "not contact them anymore," and also that they "would not refer us to other people who might be in touch with the other side."

For the first and last time in our history, the psychic community has let Good Boy Magazine down. We now know that psychics are untrustworthy, and you tarot card people are on notice.

So here is our last-ditch effort to learn from this titan of comics history. We bought the oldest Ouija board in our price range we could find on eBay, turned off the lights, and asked our questions directly...

to the spirit of Mr. Charles "Sparky" Schulz.

- Is the atelier in the afterlife comfortable?

- Do you like to draw?

- I haven't the foggiest what colon cancer is. Was it embarrassing to die that way?

- If you were an animal

what would you be?

- Are there internet cafes after death? If not, how do you pirate movies? Are you just stuck watching the same old VHS of 1987's Baby Boom you bootlegged to heaven?

- Did you always want to be a cartoonist?

Were you a huge disappointment to your parents?

- Did you watch a lot of TV on earth?

- Have you been to McDonalds recently? They're selling ugly snoopies/snorges books that are credited as written by you.

- What was the most embarrassing idea for a comic you had but didn't draw or threw away?

In the style of his famous comic strip, he said nothing. We are left to wander this harsh world on our own. Is Charles too much of a coward to answer us, or is he leaving us to answer these universal questions in our own way? Much like Lucy, he pulls the football away at the last minute, our bodies spiraling through the void and crashing to the earth, without answers and even more questions bearing down on our already overtaxed minds. We cry out for answers to the void. On this day, we are all Snoopy.

@#$!
420 FAKE Street
BY ALEX KROKUS

alright
let's get settled
BULL SHIT
CRAP

takka takka
LOFI BEATS TO SLACK OFF TO

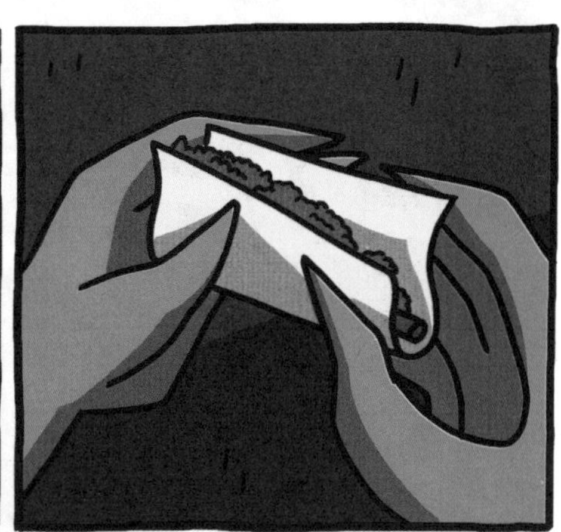

bmm
psh
bm
psh

KRAK!!!

LOOK WHAT YOU MADE ME DO!!!!

!

NILES WTF

DOES A CLOSED DOOR MEAN ANYTHING TO YOU?!!

you broke the showerhead in Benny's room...
what?!
i didn't even know we had a third bathroom!
jeez. breaking a showerhead on move-in day. that's quite a first impression to make, Claire...
i said i didn't do it...
don't worry! we'll just use your security deposit to fix-
SHIT!!

yo Beth
sup? trash bagel?
PNK

just found 'em!
ah im good
hey are all of our room mates as asisinine as Niles?
uh
...as in like... eccentric?

BETH DO YOU KNOW WHAT YR FRIEND DID TO BENNY'S BEDROOM?!
BETH I DIDN'T!

Niles i don't know and i don't care
FUCK YOU BOTH!
HEY FUCK YOU!

siouxsie, open up!!

KNOCK KNOCK

TURN THAT SHIT OFF AND ANSWER MY QUESTIONS! YOU ARE A SUSPECT IN THE FLOODING OF BENNY'S BEDROOM

hey Benny

hey guys

you uh sleepin outside again?
outside?

...haha yeah i guess i was

shutup! shut up! Benny don't listen to a single lie that they're spewing!

okay Niles!

Benny, Siouxsie and i agree that Claire should give me her security deposit because she and Beth flooded your bedroom...
sounds fair
Benny, neither of us flooded your bedroom!
Niles probably did it...

oh, that's cool, man
Benny, i would never

hey listening to Niles lie is fun but i think it's more important that we fix the leak before our kitchen ceiling caves in

oh god! we should have the landlord look at it when he comes to collect rent today...

hey, where's my joint?
SLAM!

Cynthia!
hi Niles! have you found your rent check for the past two months yet?

wow you look really really awful
Claire and Beth broke the shower head in Benny's bedroom
CHK

i'm gonna need Claire's security deposit to do the repairs myself

afterwards, i can pay back the rent that i owe
sounds like something the landlord should do. we should have a house meeting about it
yo Cynthia!
do you have the landlord's nu-
house meeting!
RIGHT NOW!
NILES WTF!

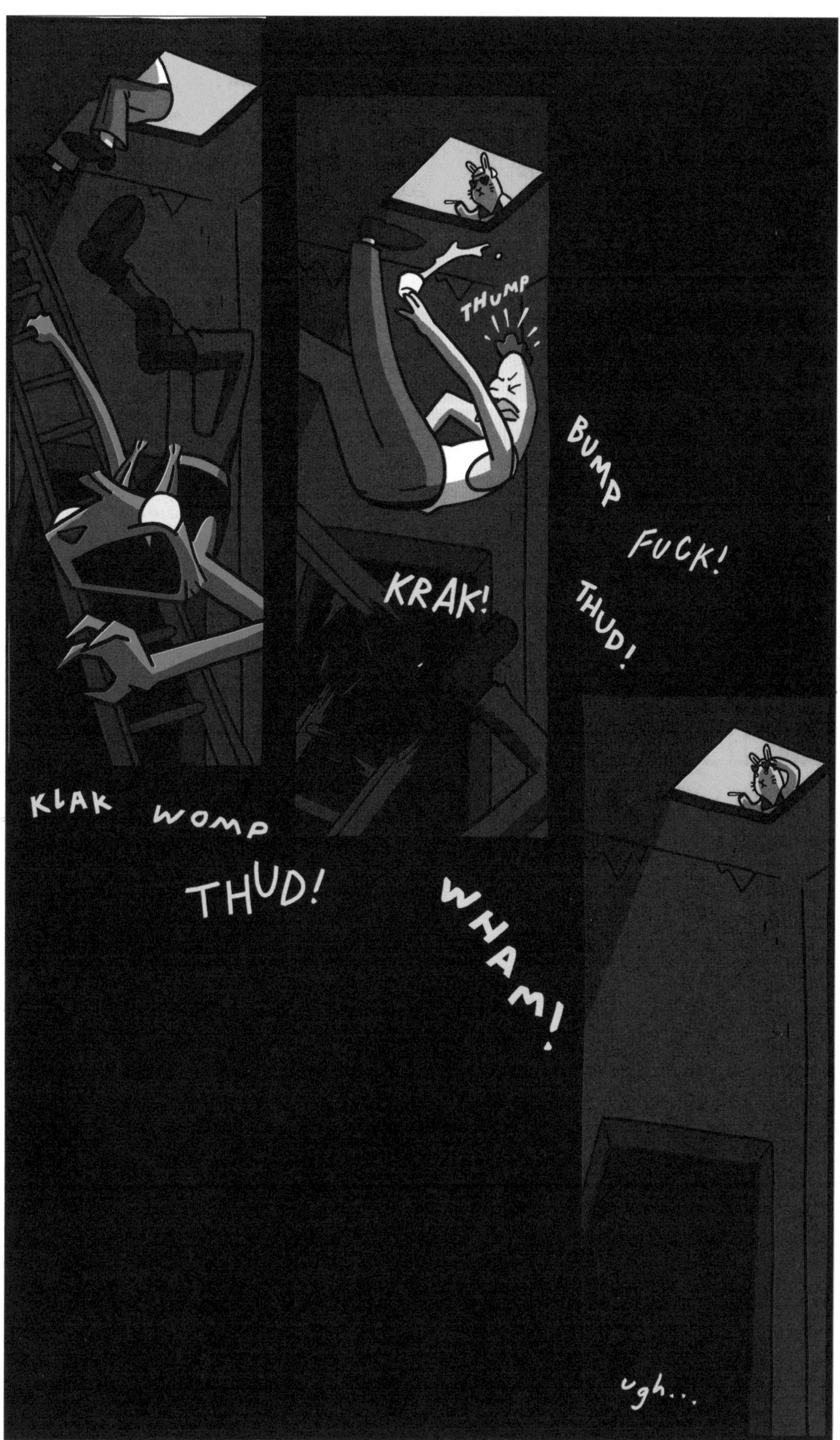
THUMP
BUMP
FUCK!
KRAK!
THUD!
KLAK
WOMP
THUD!
WHAM!
ugh...

most of us know why we're here
this is a waste of time

quiet you

why is it raining inside?

because someone here isn't taking responsibility...

for the harm they've caused you, Benny
oh

does anyone else think it's weird that Niles is insisting i pay him with my security deposit?
to install one showerhead?
PNK!

maybe Niles is tryna pay off his rent with Claire's security deposit...
Beth, it's fine if Niles broke the showerhead. mistakes happen.
will anyone be here tonight if the landlord comes to look at it?
thank you, Siouxsie!

Cynthia, i'm looking out for the house
our community!
by embezzling my security deposit on my move-in day?!
chill, Claire. we all think he's full of shit
PNK

et tu, Benny?
what?
oh, i'm good man.
i got this bagel
PNK

Niles, if you did flood Benny's room to pay off your debts with Claire's security deposit, maybe it would feel good to admit it?
sigh
PNK
PNK
PNK
PNK

...
alright-
BKSH!

KREEEEEEEEEE

WOOMFSH!

KRAK!!!
end
thx

I'VE BEEN USING THIS NEW MEDITATION APP.
CLICK

I'M TAKING THE COURSE ON HOW TO BURN SHIT WITH MY MIND.
REAL HEAD
SMOOTH BRAIN
BURN SHIT
FORGIVE DAD
LUV URSELF
EGG DEATH
BEEP
BOOP
Bestie

INHALE

EXHALE

SOUND DANGEROUS? SOUND KOOKY?
WELL, THE APP SAYS THAT BY THE TIME I LEARN HOW TO BURN SHIT I WONT WANT TO ANYMORE.

REMINDS ME OF A STORY ABOUT A SAGE FROM EARTH.

THEY SAY SHE LEARNED TO MOVE MOUNTAINS...

BY ACCEPTING THAT THE MOUNTAINS WERE ALREADY EXACTLY WHERE THEY NEEDED TO BE.

I THINK IT'LL BE DIFFERENT FOR ME THO...

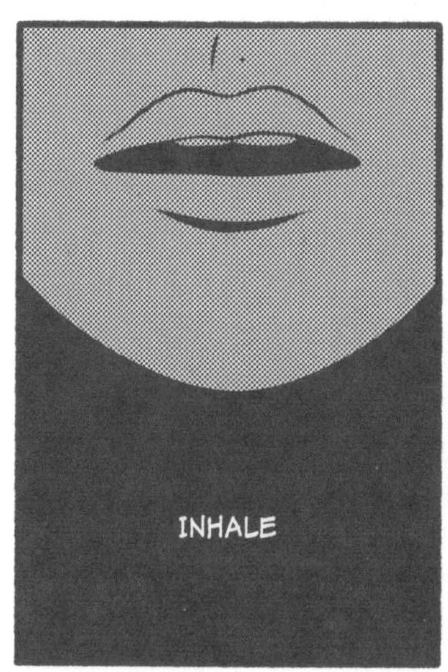
INHALE

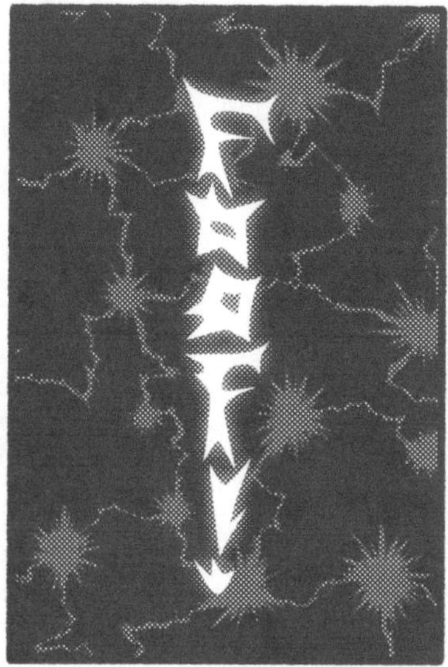
FOOF!

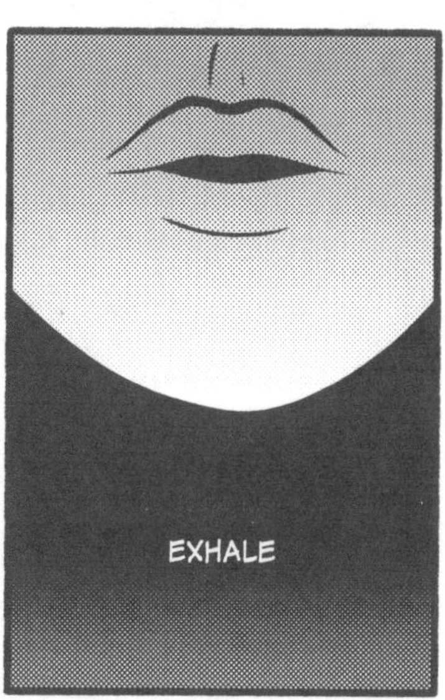
EXHALE

I REALLY WANNA BURN SHIT.

Benji Nate | 2
girlbenji.com

Flower Alligator | 12
floweralligator.com

Konstantinos Moutzouvis | 17
@korakonero

Daniel Rinylo | 25
@dan_rinylo

Dave Mercier | 28
mercworks.net

Sam Grinberg | 37
samgrinberg.com

Bastian Najdek | 44
@getxxlost

Steve Thueson | 47
stevethueson.com

Joseph Romagano | 67
@theundertaker90

Michael Sweater | 75
michaelsweater.com

Ashley Robin Franklin | 93
arfranklinstein.com

Alex Krokus | 106
@alexkrokus

Grayson Bear | 120
graysonbear.com

READ MORE FROM SILVER SPROCKET

SILVERSPROCKET.NET